HANDFUL OF SALT

مشتێ خوێ

HANDFUL OF SALT

Kajal Ahmad

translated from the Kurdish by

Alana Marie Levinson-LaBrosse
Mewan Nahro Said Sofi
Darya Abdul-Karim Ali Najm
Barbara Goldberg, Series Editor

INTERNATIONAL EDITIONS
THE WORD WORKS
WASHINGTON, D.C

The Word Works
P.O. Box 42164
Washington, D.C. 20015
editor@wordworksbooks.org

Cover art: "Meditation" by Lukman Ahmad
Cover design: Susan Pearce
Kajal Ahmad photograph: compliments of the poet
Photographs of translators:
Alana Marie Levinson-LaBrosse by Jack Looney
Mewan Nahro Said Sofi, Darya Abdul-Karim Ali Najm,
& Barbara Goldberg by Alana Marie Levinson-LaBrosse

LCCN: 2016934568
ISBN: 978-1-944585-03-7

Acknowledgments

The following poems have appeared previously as listed:

In Their Own Words (The Poetry Society of America): translations of and essays on "Were I a Martyr," "Buttons," "In the Country of Terror," and "Mirror."

Loch Raven Review: "A Single Strand of Hair," "A Small One, Sadly, Grows Up," "Ah, You Don't See Me," "Handful of Salt."

Notre Dame Review: "Our Holocaust."

Words Without Borders: "Separation from Earth" (earlier version).

The following poems have been excerpted: "*No*," "More Tender Than Mariam," "The N's of Negative," "27 Years of Suicide," "An Excerpt from the Story of My Heart," "Our Holocaust," "In the Country of Terror."

CONTENTS

∞

PREFACE

In ancient times, defeated cities were razed to the ground and the surrounding fields sown with salt. This laid waste to the land, rendering it desolate and barren.

Yet salt can heal. It preserves and purifies. It enhances flavor, is an essential component of blood. Tears of grief can restore wholeness. In many religions there is a "covenant of salt" between man and God. Sharing bread and salt in the Muslim tradition is the basis of hospitality, a rite of friendship.

In the translations that *Handful of Salt* offers, Kurdish poet Kajal Ahmad explores these multiple aspects of salt, both its destructive and healing power. Her words, like knives, dig deep, peel away the tough outer skin of Kurdish custom and culture, laying bare her vulnerable heart.

She holds nothing back: her rage is intense, her love is intense, especially her love of homeland, bruised and battered from without and within. In her poem "*No*," she writes:

> ...I can't separate
> myself from Kurdistan:
> ...In destruction's wake
> we look alike. Burning
> gathers us, wounds gather us,
> conscience gathers us, frailty
> and suffering and madness gather us.

Ahmad is a woman who so closely identifies with her homeland that she feels its every wound as her own: in "Godless Snow" she asks, "Why is there no end? My liver / burns. Why is there no end? Tragedy and funerals, comedy / and parties: why is there no end?"

In a stance her area of the world makes difficult, Ahmad is both a Muslim and a feminist. Much of her rage is directed against the rigid patriarchal culture of her country, how, as in "Two Chairs," it "sits" on her: "a Middle Eastern man sits... / in my head.... / he shatters me— / he sits—"

But Ahmad is also angry at the women of Kurdistan for not asserting their rights, for passively accepting the only two roles a male-dominated society has deemed appropriate: wife and mother. In "*No*," Ahmad envisions a time when women assume a more powerful role. "Ah, how I resent our mothers. The female / partridge knows her sex, but our girls, / our women don't. It will take / my mother to act as my father...." And again, in "Verge of Doubt," she asks, "...how can you say / it's normal for girls to live only / for marriage and childbirth, / servant by day, plaything by night?"

It is not that Ahmad doesn't have tender feelings for men, even one man in particular. But she is clear where her deepest affection lies: her poetry. In "A Single Strand of Hair," she states, "I don't want / any darling apart / from pen, page, line." This devotion comes with sacrifice—no enduring domestic relationship, no children of her own.

Ahmad's themes of injustice, gender discrimination, and the struggle between art and life mirror those of contemporary women worldwide. But Ahmad's struggles play out against the harsh backdrop of Kurdish tradition and history, largely unknown in the West.

During the brutal Iran-Iraq War (1980-1988), Saddam Hussein's use of chemical warfare left a bitter legacy, contaminating the land the Kurds inhabited in Northern Iraq. It became a wasteland, harking back to ancient times when fields were strewn with salt. Thousands of Kurdish civilians were killed, many set off on foot for safer ground and in the years following the attacks, more died from disease and suffered birth defects. These horrific events are known as *Anfal*, what the Kurds call "our holocaust." Its legacy exerts a powerful grip on Ahmad's psyche. In "Our Holocaust," she explains:

> That history: bright sugar dissolving
> in the toxic dark. The rose
> surrendered, became a thistle.
> The nation that forgets its Anfal
> is beheaded.

And she doesn't want to forget this legacy, nor coat it with honey. But how to live with it, to maintain a free and independent spirit? How to live with wounds that are an intimate part of her personal history?

Thankfully, not all is despair. Some of Ahmad's poems exhibit a playful spirit. She has memories of joy, that time in childhood when even the mothers wore short, red skirts, reminding us that Kurdish women were not always so oppressed, nor men so harsh and judgmental. It was a time when her imagination flourished, when the world was green, seen in "A Small One, Sadly, Grows Up":

> In the past
> I had no season that was not
> vibrant. I chased garden frogs
> on my knees. I thought
> the world was made up
> of the secret life of frogs,
> their confessions...

Of course that innocence did not last. In the same poem she writes, "When we were children / we played hide-and-seek / with them, these boys / who now have guards, beat their wives, / are thieves, murderers, martyrs."

As Series Editor of The Word Works International Editions, I am always on the lookout for quality manuscripts in translation. There is no dearth. But finding one like this, teeming with rage, sorrow, and tenderness, one that stays true to the voice and tone of the original, in short, one I could love—that is rare. I find Ahmad's wild, strange and absolutely unique imagery irresistible. Take this one example: "Separation from Earth":

> When I exploded
> my hair like the horizon
> became a belt around Earth's
> waist. I turned myself
> into a pair of socks
> for the South Pole...

And I could not resist the poems themselves, ferocious yet loving. They afford us entry into a mysterious corner of the world, off the main stage of history, though today Kurdish fighters, the *peshmerga*, are frequently in the headlines. As of this writing, they are the only "boots on the ground" that have had military successes in the fight against ISIS. This makes it even more essential that we accord them the courtesy, the respect of learning more about their history and character.

The notion of hospitality in Middle Eastern culture is well known. Still, how freely Ahmad opens her home to us. We are welcomed not as distant relatives, but as intimate friends. Her poems envelop us. We feel their warmth, passion, and intensity. She offers us bread sprinkled with salt. And we gratefully accept.

Barbara Goldberg
Washington, D.C.

INTRODUCTION

Kajal Ahmad (b. 1967) came of age as one of Iraqi Kurdistan's
leading feminists. Saddam Hussein rose to power in her early
childhood. Under threat from his snipers, she distributed leaflets
for Kurdish political movements. As a young woman, she began
writing poetry and working as a journalist. During the Kurdish
Uprising (1991) and the Kurdish Civil War (1994-1997), she
served as a correspondent from the front lines, a member of the
peshmerga, Kurdish guerilla forces. When she began to read her
poetry publicly, the response was overwhelming. Women, especially,
would attend her readings in the hundreds and thousands. As
Ahmad says, they found each other's pain and spoke without veils.

Ahmad spoke in traditional language to address customs she saw
as outmoded. She drew on proverbs and colloquial Kurdish, using
the familiar to talk about the unfamiliar: possibilities for women
and Kurdish society. Ahmad spoke plainly about virginity and its
costs, about desire, about the relationship between the sexes. To
many, her honesty was as dirty as curse words. They compared her
to the famous (and infamous) Sheikh Raza Talabani, a 19th century
poet who combined art and invective. The Lady Sheikh Raza, they
called her, and she bore the name as an honorific. Many more were
drawn to the spirit, fire, and hope the poems contained. These
readers could feel that, as she says, she has lived the words and is
dedicated to the beloved, to Kurdistan.

Kurdistan is a national idea that has been only partially realized.
Kurds as an ethnic group number approximately 35 million people,
spread across Turkey, Syria, Iraq, and Iran. Since the dissolution
of the Ottoman Empire, with the emergence of modern nations
in the region, Kurds have agitated for an independent state of
their own. In so doing, they have suffered systematic persecution
across their ancestral lands. In Turkey, in an attempt to create a
monolithic Turkish identity, the state banned manifestations of

Kurdishness, including dress and language. These bans, militarily enforced, lasted over a hundred years and were only recently lifted. To the south, in Iraq, Saddam Hussein tried to eradicate Kurdish identity. He instituted *Anfal* (1986-1989), a campaign of ethnic slaughter that aimed to kill all Kurdish men of military age. Chemical weapons were deployed in the course of these operations. Halabja, the city at the center of this extensive bombing, now falls within the borders of the semi-autonomous Kurdish Regional Government (KRG) and hosts a museum commemorating the tragedy. Kajal Ahmad was nineteen years old when these attacks began and living in Sulaimani, not two hours away from Halabja. She was twenty-two when the attacks concluded. She joined the uprising at twenty-four.

Perhaps because Kurds have existed outside the mechanics of the modern state, poetry continues to offer a way to nurture cultural identity. Poet and reader share a powerful civic bond in Kurdistan, a mostly ethereal country. The poet is trusted as a voice in society, working to clarify and cut through, to perceive what others don't or won't, to show the world as it may or ought to be. Readings are still widely attended—even small readings draw crowds in the hundreds—and audiences, having memorized the poems, often mouth them along with the poet. Kajal Ahmad forged this bond with her readers. Through years of reporting, writing, and even hosting her own television show, she became a radical, stalwart voice for women's rights.

I discovered her work when I moved to northern Iraq to lecture at the American University of Iraq, Sulaimani (AUIS). In a city of over a million people that is sometimes called "The Paris of Kurdistan," all the main roads are named for the people's poets. The tradition of Kurdish poetry is wide and deep and largely untranslated. The poetry of Iraq, more broadly considered, is rich with classical and contemporary poets and writers worthy of translation. I wanted to read these writers and discover the literary world my students knew so well.

My students were ready for the work. The student population is diverse and multi-lingual. Every student is fluent in English and the vast majority has command of at least one other language: Arabic, Kurdish, Farsi, and Turkish are most common. When I offered a literary translation workshop, students were enthusiastic and wonderfully qualified. The workshop became an annual offering. I taught students ways to bring their favorite authors into English and they introduced me to the luminaries in Iraqi and Kurdish poetry.

Darya Abdul-Karim Ali Najm and Mewan Nahro Said Sofi, co-translators on this manuscript, were both students in that workshop. They introduced me to Kajal Ahmad's poetry, and together we studied how Kajal constructed her concepts of womanhood, how we might build our own. Translating these poems was as much about language, image, and meaning as it was about womanhood, though Ahmad says, "I believe in women in literature, but I don't work for that. It's not my project. It just occurs." The act of translating these poems was one such occurrence: it brought us together—the woman behind the poems and the women behind the translations. Barbara Goldberg, Series Editor of The Word Works International Editions, became a co-translator, joining us as another woman who believes in these poems. Like Ahmad, I didn't set out to work for women in literature, but one great joy of these poems seems to be the people who gather around them. Said Sofi, Ali Najm, and Goldberg, like the poet we have come to know, are vibrant, intelligent, and delightfully wild.

We have come to know a woman in these poems who many feel no longer exists. To many, Kajal Ahmad is not who she once was. In 2008, the feminist icon who had loved men openly, loved her country passionately, and spoken out against the headscarf, married a wealthy, conservative Jordanian man (Kurdish by heritage), moved to Amman, and took the hijab. Women in her home country were angered, confused, and dismayed. Ahmad's choices felt like betrayal.

Almost a decade later, the poet speaks about her apparently retrograde decisions. Fame may have seemed desirable as a young woman, but it came to be a great burden. Cultivating the image of a public icon was brutal. Men desired her, but none would openly love her or marry her. Women admired her, but always at a distance. People clapped for her or denounced her, but none drew close. She saw that she had cast off so many elements of traditional feminine identity that, freed of that weight, she had drifted too far beyond the vanguard. "I wouldn't have become the poet I am without this pressure," she says, and yet, being the icon cost her too much. "Women who have gone through what I have, they either die, give everything up, or find a way to make space." The hijab, she says, is part of having someone in her life she wants, but it has "cracked" her image as an author and a leader. She isn't inured to the disappointment her readers feel, she feels the bitterness of this choice, but she also has faith that, "What stays in the future are my poems. The scarf will go. I will go. My poems will stay. What I am is my poems. Everything else is far away."

Different as she may now seem, the woman I have met is the woman of her poems. Over tea, in Jordan and in Iraq, we have discussed her verses and her life. Whatever veil she wears has not dropped over her mind or her speech. She returned to Sulaimani as the Islamic State threatened her people, her land, and the progress for which she and others of her generation have worked. As hard times again came to her country, she wanted to be home. Kurdistan, she explained to me, is a hard-hearted lover. You give everything to him and sometimes he loves you back. You don't love him to have the love returned. You love because he is worth loving. The freedom she fought for is not the freedom the country has achieved today. Women still die in honor-killings. People still rise through personal connection, not intellectual merit. She stops. It's painful to speak poorly of your lover.

Yet, speaking as she does from within the veil is as powerful, and to some, perhaps more so, than unveiled. Mostly, she is a survivor of the bitterness that often comes with publicly living out the questions of the contemporary feminist in Iraq and Kurdistan. The image of the icon has cracked, but the woman remains, and she has so much left to tell us.

Alana Marie Levinson–LaBrosse
Exeter, England

About the Translation

I learned Kurdish from translating poetry. Each poet leans into certain rhythms in Kurdish, showing me ways the language can move. When I first began translating Kajal Ahmad's poetry, I would often stumble through her sentences. Her syntax coils in on itself like rope. She plays with the ambiguity made possible in Kurdish by the way it structures adjectives. Attributes, time, possession, location, and relationship can all be heaped on top of each other in word-piles: "the year of the genocide of the descendants of butterflies." In Kurdish, all she has to do is add "y" to the end of each word. English resists that habit. Prepositions used that way in English would be vague, a tangle. It's too cumbersome: all that "of the."

As translators, we tried to preserve her use of phrases traditional to Kurdish that are highly tactile, rarely abstract. The most common greeting in Iraqi Kurdistan is "Serchow," or, "Above my eyes." Popular endearments are "My liver," "My breath." In Kurdish, one doesn't say, "You disappoint me." One says, "You're breaking my hands." Forgiveness becomes the physical gesture of loosing someone's neck from your strangling hands. One is not killed, but loses his head. In "More Tender than Mariam," Mariam doesn't know God; she has seen his armpits. The poet isn't full or overflowing with images and ideas. She has lips within lips. Ahmad leans again and again into this linguistic pattern of Kurdish to create a world that happens in the body, to the body. The world is both intimate and threatening. The body is vulnerable and enduring.

In most instances, we endeavored to keep this kind of language. In others, where fidelity to the most literal meaning of a word would interfere with understanding, we chose simplicity. The Kurdish word for coffin, for instance, is "tree / wood of corpses." Fantastic. But in the poem "Godless Snow," we worried that literal translation would change the image, that the reader would no longer see a single coffin, but an extended lineage of death, a family tree of corpses. In this case, we thought a less literal translation would serve the poem better.

Finally, as mentioned above, Kurds throughout the regions they inhabit (Turkey, Syria, Iraq, Iran, and small areas of Armenia) have suffered systematic physical and cultural persecution for over a hundred years. While other ethnicities have been able to codify their languages, create dictionaries, thesauruses, and grammars, Kurds have routinely been banned from speaking their language, forcibly relocated, and for Iraqi Kurds, Arabized. Within the relative protection of the semi-autonomous zone of the KRG, linguistic freedom has blossomed, bringing with it a new wave of reference texts. That said, these texts are still in the early stages and none are definitive. Many older or rarer words poets use cannot be found in dictionaries and must be scouted out in conversation with experts in the language or older speakers who might still be familiar with almost-antiquated usage.

This makes translation of Kurdish poetry a highly social endeavor. Said Sofi, Ali Najm, and I learned our communities as we translated these verses. The readers and speakers around us were patient and, above all, understanding. Often, we asked for a word's meaning without knowing if the answer would be embarrassing. For example, Grandma is often the only one who might know that "a red face" is a traditional way to refer not to blushing, but to proof of a bride's virginity. All those around us, including grandmas, fathers, mothers, cousins, and friends, treated these moments with humor and a gentle professionalism. We are very grateful.

Our use of many sources, however, meant that we encountered many different answers to our questions. In Ahmad's poem "No," does she mean to say "fertile" or "sudden" breast? In cases of dispute, we looked to the poem's context for resolution. Often, it was relatively obvious. We suppose a breast could be sudden, but it is much more likely to be fertile. We know not everyone will agree with our choices, and we welcome alternative views. Undoubtedly we've missed certain perspectives, but translation is never finished and publication is less a final result than the beginning of a much wider conversation.

Alana Marie Levinson-LaBrosse

Separation from Earth ~ down

When I exploded
my hair like the horizon
became a belt around Earth's
waist. I turned myself
into a pair of socks
for the South Pole.
For the North I wove
a hat and jamana*
from the threads of my soul.
Land was sick of me:
it wanted to tear me off
like an old coat. I hung myself
on its beard, its mercy
but Earth cast me into the arms
of the universe. I became
a star in the sky and now
I have my own place and my own
desires and I am denser
with lives than Earth.

BECOMING A MARTYR

I want no flowers,
no evening of union,
no dawn of parting.
I want no flowers
for out of my body
blossom the loveliest flowers.
I want no kisses
unless from the strongest,
most handsome of men—
no evening of marriage, no
dawn of a woman newly widowed.
I want no kisses
if I am martyred for love.
I want no tears
over the coffin or my corpse.
I want no pity, no Judas tree
dragged to the walls of my grave,
no flowers nor kisses,
no tears nor miseries.
Bring nothing.
Hold nothing.
I die as a homeland without flag,
without voice.
I am grateful.
I want nothing.
I will accept nothing.

No

A wild horse inside me gallops
and neighs in the breeze.
What good is it? For women today
is a stone age. I wish my eyes
could make it end, no need
to explode, to burst
into laughter, tears. It's simple
to find melody in a glance, dance
while still, sing in symbols, but speech
is heavy, a nest of tongues, no shelter
for egg and fledgling. The snake
in my throat has come to feast.

Ah, how I resent our mothers. The female
partridge knows her sex, but our girls,
our women don't. It will take
my mother to act as my father.
Mother-Father, tell me what
to say. What's said in the streets
beheads me. Father, without
my consent you brought me into
your world of mustache and hookah,
Father, Baba.*

My land rejects me in the womb.
Even as contractions press my head,
you prepare to bury me alive, day
after day, you erase me. *No.*
Forever, *No.* After all this
death, I remain.

In the room of my mother's belly
live coals fill me—
my poetry is fire, my breath

is fire, my affection, Zoroastrian.
When I get older, they will
pour soil on my wounds:
my blood will be soil.

Women and Kurdistan:
how similar we are, how
strange. I can't separate
myself from Kurdistan:
we're soil and soil, fire and fire,
water and water, how heavy
it is. In destruction's wake
we look alike. Burning
gathers us, wounds gather us,
conscience gathers us, frailty
and suffering and madness gather us.
Why are we one in *No*?

I and my Kurdistan, how heavy,
we can't come together as one.

Windows are paned with all
that's left unsaid, windows on windows.
Now I am filled with speech and worry
and worry. Torture fills me up, lip to lip.
One by one, I'll open you, windows
of what's unsaid, windows on windows.

1. Against What's Against

Flowers are made to live
with thorns: how my heart burns
for those flowers. Shade was forced
to wed the sun: my heart burns
for the shade. A marauder cloaked in pitch

black night won't let the luminous
girl be. My heart burns.

If you were a flower, you'd suffer
no thorn. If you were shade
you'd divorce the sun, and if
you were light you would be.

2. Politics of Roosters

Outside it sings:
a rooster on a clothesline.
No one listens to the call
to prayer. A man's voice
empties a clip of curses.
The rooster sings. Another clip.
The rooster sings and sings.
How dumb he is. Why doesn't he
go back to sleep? So
say I, the chicken.

3. Fading

My lunacy is not sudden or random.
One morning, my Hama Dok* said,
"You're the most beautiful among
the mad." I clapped with laughter
for that little moment. Hunger
and thirst and agony flow out.
The mirror of my body is obscured
by dust from deserts, politics, country.
I'm fading into madness, but I don't
say, "How am I beautiful, Hama Dok?"
Fading away: how is that beauty?

4. The Insanity of Existence

I die for Kurdistan. Its patriots won't
let it be *my* Kurdistan. In a land
of men, under a sky of men, under
a God of men, how did this *No*
grow to my height? Where are
the winged branches, leaves, and roots
of this blind tree, this *No* tree
of mine? I am flooded with *No*: this
is the rain of conscience and season
of loathing. Come. Welcome.

A carnival of corpses, women and girls,
unleash their ululation to welcome
the last gasp of reticence.
In a stone age, *No*
is a ray and a miracle.

From here on, I am the smallest
among you, a prophet not chosen
by God, a surprise
to my mother, to a conjurer,
to a homeland, a people.
Stone me now
then no one will doubt my prophecy.
Put down stepping-stones
for questioning believers
to follow my path.

I waited for my father to wed
my mother. I waited to be born.
I was my own midwife. I bit
my own umbilical cord.

From here on, I am an ocean
of refusal, a birthplace
of complaint. I am this
year's season of discord. Together
take refuge under my abundant hair,
succor at my fertile breast.

WALKING SAHOLAKA

If we want to walk in the rain
together, we take a shower
with our clothes on, if
we want to walk arm in arm
in Saholaka,* we close our eyes
and are on our way. I whisper,
"Why do you look at girls?"
You say, "Let's just close
our eyes. Let's just walk."
We bump into the sweet seller's
window. Our noses—we snap out of it—
are pressed against our own
window. We see out to the forbidden
garden. We rush to close
the curtain and sit together
on a single chair.

This is the end of the sad love story
I finished for him and now read.

Handful of Salt

Every day, hoping
he would leave, I poured
a handful of salt* in the shoe
of the irresolute man
I once loved greatly.

I knew, so far as I could
tell, that this visitor
would kill me and my poems.
His timing was unfortunate.

DIRECTION

In the mountains, wherever
he took his shoes* off, they pointed
toward the city. He didn't hope
this meant the homeland
would be set free.

Now, in the city, wherever he puts
his shoes, they point abroad, but
he doesn't dream that one day
without the mirage of the foreign
world he imagines, without direction
from his shoes, he will travel
through the heart
of his country, preserve
mythology inside his
grandmother's hope chest,
bury that under
a happy home and close
several doors, colorful
as the covers of childhood
fairytales, over it.

A Small One, Sadly, Grows Up

As a small one I hid myself
under the leaves of the rubber tree.
I was that small.
On the top step, the highest,
I sat estranged. In secret,
a book read me and I read
a book. My cheeks blushed
from shyness. Each evening,
poetry wrote me. I got bigger.
The rubber tree hid itself in me.
On the highest step, I still
wait, estranged. A book
reads me and I read a book.
Now, as then, shyness grips me
when a poem writes me,
when I write a poem.
Fate is a curse that will never let me
return to my small self, the beautiful
self that is gone.
They call it growing up. You,
my eyes, do you know? In the past
I had no season that was not
vibrant. I chased garden frogs
on my knees. I thought
the world was made up
of the secret life of frogs,
their confessions. Now
I have no time to chase
fantasies. Who is more ignorant
than the man with no time to sink
to his knees and chase frogs, immersed
as he is in global trade?
How simple are the dreams of water
where it begins:

a village girl with a jar on her shoulders
understands them.
Not once a year do I dream.
I am jealous of water—
also of the jar—
also of the village girl.
What kind of Tuni Baba* is this city?
When we were children
we played hide-and-seek
with them, these boys
who now have guards, beat their wives,
are thieves, murderers, martyrs.
Of some I have no news. Some
don't allow their children to play
hide-and-seek on the street
like we did.
You see?
Do you see, my eyes,
what a curse it is to grow up?

In the Country of Terror I Love Streets More than Men

The street doesn't ask, "Where
are you now?" and, "Where are you
headed, you crazy girl?" The street
isn't strict. It doesn't know terror.
Nothing of the street looks like men
and nothing of men
looks like streets.

It tells me: Go,
cross over. Grow up: love
doesn't bear the smallest burden.
Women with wings fall
when they love vain men,
callow boys. The vessel of life
shatters with your heart.

That street—I crossed it
with that someone.
Fate forbade us
from loving each other.
My heart flew when I ran
away with that someone.
He let himself lag behind
so he wouldn't pass me, so that I
could run ahead.

Just one street is enough
for freedom to rejoice, for children
to go to school, for boys to look
at girls and for girls to laugh.

A street that carries my name
should have no sculptures

of famous men. Let it be wide, let it
be wide, wide as my heart.
Let it be empty in the morning
and in the evening like the quiet
of a poem's house and let it be
noisy at other times like my insides,
lips within lips.

I need a street washed clean
of bloodstains, a street
that has never seen or known terror.
Let it be pure, pure,
pure like the sex of these girls
killed unjustly. Let it be long, long,
long as their agony.

On that street, we are all
travelers, and I will remain
a traveler. The quatrains
of Nishapur* will not suddenly trust
themselves and madly drunk
with love walk
arm in arm with me.

Ah, You Don't See Me

The other world through the window
of my current life is olive trees
and fog as far as the eyes can see.

Sadly, you don't see me, even
when I sweep olives from the trees
in autumn, even after I wash
them with exile,
sprinkle them with lemon water
and rock salt, season
them with my pain and journey,
even when I place those olives
in a clean, translucent jar

you don't see me. My hands break.
You don't see how, with the trees,
I go bare and blossom,
blossom and go bare.

When I become a bird,
and grow wings, I will
either fall from above, or
fly from below.

Ah, you don't know:
with a lover as ruthless
as my homeland
I live untouched.
I grow thorns
like a cactus
from heartbreak.

VERGE OF DOUBT

I wish to be more
than a woman, a poet
or a King of Women.
If my fame flies from one corner
of the world to another, still
my dreams will travel beyond
this world's borders or customs,
beyond maps of the other world,
beyond rusty words. Often
I reflect: how can you say
it's normal for girls to live only
by marriage and childbirth,
servant by day, plaything by night?
I approach the season of marriage.
Almighty Creator, can I brace myself
as the sword of judgment falls
from a people who reduce me
to nothing because I am no
bride to their revelry?

Beloved, you defend sharia,* but
for that, in one night I will lose
my girlhood in someone's bedclothes somewhere.
Oh, mullah,* oh, teacher of confusion,
if you only knew what virginity means
to our women, and what we do
to preserve it. It is precious, so
terribly precious. Do you think the shame
of it, the shame won't shatter me,
that my heart won't stop, when
my husband surrounded by old women
announces my red face by parading
from street to street?

Always I am on the verge
of doubt. I am my man's honor
but he is not mine. I am of his left rib
and I am Satan. By whose beard is this just?

Oh, sea, I am a wave and I am not
a wave. I am human and not human.
It is arduous.

When birds spread their wings, this universe
is too tight. How can I accept
laws that make me an idol
of lust? Oh, dear friend, if earth
and sky and weather are drenched
in love and nothing changes,
how can I be bright-sighted?
If lovers are blind to verdant splendor
how can I not fear my sex?
The size of my shadow? The touch
of our hands that will bring
these walls to their knees?
Oh, dear friend.

Buttons

Between kisses, the first
button of my pink blouse
fell off. Later, sewing,
her eyes behind her glasses,
the needle in her hand
scolding like a finger,
she spat out, "Don't you
put this in a poem!"

Woman in Whispers

From the pupil of a clouded eye,
pain whispered, "Tonight
I am a woman in labor.
If she dies, I die."

The mirror had a vision:
this woman's weariness
is that man's rest.
Until dawn, instead
of him, I will hold my tears.

Tonight: passion.
I measure the span
of my love's hands.
He watches my tears fall
away with the chains
that have rattled around
my ankles. When he dances,
I dance.

Tonight: nuptials
and white dress.

Tonight: my daughter is sick.
Inside small hands,
my heart constricts.

I am a green homeland. For how many
years has my beauty broken
your pens. No one
will record my history
nor write my anguish
in a novel.

Don't look for me
through the narrow frame
of earlier times.
I am a cloud, I pour
down love and poetry.

His glance asks,
"Where is your black hair?
When did it fall?" My silence
tells him, "I sold it
to buy a book
for you."

Life vanishes. Without
you, wolves will eat me.
Without me, you can't
bring down the sun.
Cyclones of dust engulf us.
May I not be lost.
May you not be lost.

FIND, FIND

As a child, when I lost a bead
I'd say, "Find, find, find*
it for me. It's not mine,
it's the Divine's." Now

losing you, I can't say
those words. The difference
between now and then
is this: then, I went mad
if I lost a single dream;
now, I hope I never find
what I once held in my hands.
I hide myself from wishing—
If is in my way.

The *find, find* of before
was a white lie. I don't know
what force, which person
I wanted to fool. I hid
behind the divine and waited
for a miracle.

But my lost one now belongs
to the non-divine.
On the other side of time
I have forgotten
whether to tell
the white lie
or the black.

45

A SINGLE STRAND OF HAIR

A single strand* of hair falls
on my forehead. I don't,
as my mother did, kiss it,
touch it to my eye and
smooth it back.

Each time, I pluck
the strand from the root
and press it
in an old book.
I don't want anyone
to miss me
except the old heroes.

I don't want
any darling apart
from pen, page, line.

GODLESS SNOW

Our homeland is death's comrade:
see, how many of us have fallen
in its graveyards. Our moons
can't keep pace burying
our moons. Our flowers witnessing
our flowers' corpses have not one
sob left. The sea of women's tears
has dried, split, and cracked

and now, the raven calls
my pure white martyrs
godless. Now, now, the hands
of war grip the collar, provoke
the stem and bloom, they call
my heart's bright beams
apostates. What destruction has come
to our homes? What love and bravery
protects us? Breathe in the land
after rain and you will know the scent
of martyrs, just how good it is. Listen
to the fire as it moans and you will know
the insides of our martyrs' mothers, their buzzing
pain, the carnival of hurt they hold.

Why is there no end? My liver
burns. Why is there no end?
Tragedy and funerals, comedy
and parties: why is there no end?
The coffin expands,
the windows, the entrance
of my breath, constrict.
How addicted I am to freedom:
I create life from death,
lanterns from my scars.

Why is there no end, and why
no beginning? There is no narrative
to the story of Anfal,* the home
of chemical rain, the house of wounded
Halabja.* What forbearance
has come to the chambers of our bodies
and what darkness, what surrender
from our eyes, apples,
and our noses, ovens? Each thorn
killed, each plant martyred, the funeral
is for my homeland and the wake
for a land that senselessly grows
both thorns and plants. What war breaks out
between the lines of my poems?
What peace over its skies? When
in moments of morning
I throw out the call to prayer
I stand with the godless
snow, with the godless sunlight.
Snow is peace and godlessness, too,
is a fight that grips one by the collar.
Why is there no end to the epic
poem of martyrs? Why is there
no end, the immortality of fire?

An Expedition

You are not a traveler—
you don't know
when you turn
from the path.
I glut myself on worry: you
yourself are an expedition.

I Put My Heart Somewhere

I'm sorry: my heart
is not in my chest.
I put it somewhere.
I don't know where.

You go search for it
in the public library.
You notice a reader
checking it out.

I'm sorry: my photo
exists—on the sidewalk,
on restaurant walls,
in the eyes of boys.

The roots of my name
reach everywhere. The broken
necklace of my life no one
can fix, not you, not anyone.

You can't cut out
the long tongues of gossips,
can't turn women into creators
of history, they are only mothers
to children. You can't turn a bride
into half a man. You do this
yet don't regret that you drank
the wine of my love. I'm sorry:
when I sleep alone my eyes fill
with separation. My poems are filled
with trysts between people I don't
even know. Leave me. You can't
find my lost self without
losing yourself.

Celestial Friends

One day the sun will rise
and I will have a lover
on one of the stars, a friend
in the far reaches of the universe.
Nothing of him, nothing, will be
human. I will have more and more
friends in celestial lands.

For my birthday feast they will come
to my house. They will bring me
a rare black and white photograph
from the era when Earth and Mars
and Moon were young.

It's not known what year
the photograph was taken, but
these planets and our moon
are smiling and serene.

I become more alien.
One day the sun will rise
and the sky will receive me.

Playing hide-and-seek
with fate, poetry kisses
my lips and brings me
down to earth.

NARRATIVE OF A LOVER

How ugly, the handwriting
scrawled by a lover
on life's wall. It's crooked:
for prayer, it faces *agh*, it swerves
at *oof.* The fairytale is punctured:
the beloved is not me, the author
of the verses, Nali,* is not you.
There is no punctuation
in this life that I spend
in ignorance, in dreams,
in a love and on a road
that are wrinkled as age,
blind as the mullah's voodoo.

MIRROR

The distorting mirror of my time broke
because it made what was small big
and what was big small.
Dictators and monsters filled its face.
Even now when I breathe
its shards stick into the walls of my heart
and instead of sweat
I leak glass.

27 Years of Suicide

That neighborhood held fragrant
memories. Perfume can never
be re-collected, or I would fill
the empty bottle to the lip. My old friends
lived there, my martyred friends,
traitors, those who left me
and a hundred times left
our homeland: they forgot us
like names of the dead.

In that neighborhood youth
endured, we remained forever
children, virginity rising
like kites, happiness chewed like gum.
Back then my girl friends granted
kisses and I...nothing. That's why
all distrusted the voice in my poems.
No...they were not wrong.

Those days I bound my breasts
and hid my hair under a grey cap.
Those seasons at our house being
a woman was a shame. I dressed
in traditional Kurdish jacket
and pants, and when we traveled
from one village to another I refused
to ride a donkey. I have spent
half my days behind doors.

In that neighborhood, I whirled
like a dervish for Komala,* but
ideology ignores personal dreams.
During meetings we discussed
everything but our defects.

54

My identity card says,
Kajal Ahmad Saeed
7/30/67, Kirkuk.
That name, that date, that place,
none of it is true. This is:
Kajal Ahmad—how readers know me,
7/14/67—my father's mistake,
Sulaimani—not Kirkuk.

Catastrophe, war, the sin
is not mine. That poetry gives
me wings is not a crime. I am
devoted to the moon, which offers
me words, keeps me alive.

That neighborhood held fragrant
memories. Then the horizon
was infinite, now the wind
is without promise like men,
water vague like women,
soil deceptive like men, fire
dishonest like women.

Come morning, I sweep
the attic and collect laundry
from the fraying clothes line.
I wash dishes, I wash
the house, I wash myself.
My rustling hem wakes
the house, which eats breakfast
and sleeps again.

On the porch, I write this epic. Silence
like this won't come again.

In that neighborhood, there once
was poetry to live for, love to die for,
brothers fought and made up,
bleeding slowed to a trickle, evil
was never this fierce, this rampant.

How long will it take to appease
those I angered? To forget
the others, delicate
as my little sister's neck?
This not-God is drunk: that's why
the world can't catch a moment
of peace. The Shahriyar*
of my love story is Adam: he knows
my whole life is suicide
and without even listening,
he kills my song, me.

Dogs

The sea of my poems yields.
All those who cheat drown
into the deep night. Dogs bark
at the moon, but the moon,
like me, is on the far ceiling
of the sky. The dogs, low
as the enemies of man, observe.

The sea of my love yields
and I don't know why, but I feel
sorry for the dogs. I throw them
a piece of my soul.
They fall to licking the earth.

Waves trouble the sea in my heart.
In the crease between lines I cry
for what dogs do. The sea stills.
I say, "God, don't You
hold it against them.
They are dogs."

More Tender Than Mariam

Oh, Mariams of my country, in times
when death is necessary,
let us mothers welcome it first,
not our children.

The nation is lonely
as Adam before
the fertile arrival of Eve.
I, too, am alone. Boredom
springs open in my heart
but I don't tire. My warm laughter,
like bread, molds. Oh, poets,
I have held two lives, but I haven't
miscarried my poem, nor
has poetry miscarried me.
When will Jesus come?
I am falling from Sirat,*
the bridge of waiting.

At the monastery of love and poems, I wept.
Algae caught at the gutter's edge of my tears.

Without poems, still
my eyes look down
the road, I wait for the way,
I wait for you. Without reason
I speak. It's never clear to me
whether I talk for you, about
the earth, or about myself.

After gagging, you were a shaft of light
in the mouth, wounded. You poured
from my mouth. Even after
your birth, I bled internally

58

with words. Did blood make me
a poet or Mariam,
the mad poet?

I secured the bridge of forgiveness
between the land of my heart and
the sky of your scalp.
Departure from myself continues.
Do you think it will depart from me for good?

You hadn't been born,
but the cross searched for you, hollow
by hollow. Had I known
it would not be tender with you
I'd have said at your birth, "Come, return
to the calm body of your mother."
Had I known they would name you
the Son of God, I wouldn't have given
you life. God can't be father
to a son if I've never spent
a single night with him. Or,
if I have laid in his arms, why
call me virgin?

Light of my eyes, you
yourself ask who
is more immaculate, Mariam
or me? Who more in love?
Is my heart's wound
deeper than her sorrow?
I say nothing. You speak yourself.
Light of my eyes, enchanted
Khunigar,* my Jesus,
don't call me Mariam the Poet or
I will bruise. As a mother,

I am more tender than Mariam.
Mariam and I, our difference
is this: even blinded, I wouldn't
close my eyes until
with my life I purchase yours.
I won't walk the footpaths of satisfaction
until I am nailed to the cross in your place.

Our difference is here: I can't,
as she did, give you up, even
to the hands of God. My heart
won't allow it. God has not seen motherhood.
He can't burn for you, his stomach can't burn
with grief. Motherhood is a vast sorrow.
I became a mother before
I became a woman.

When I created Jesus, I didn't care
if they stabbed me, or
interrogated me about my virginity.
Jesus of the earth, Jesus of the father,
I exist to uncover the lie
the world told. I won't wait
for your death. This time,
my only child, instead of your grim,
white-haired guitar, hold the corpse
of your mother. I will
die before you. My lap
will not hold your death.

Let Baghdad Come to Halabja

Let Halabja's tear-stained
kerchief wash the forehead
of Baghdad. Let him stand
ashamed at the gate
of the martyred city.

Halabja won't go to Baghdad,
let Baghdad come to Halabja
the way the world does,
faint with need
to honor those sacred graves.
How can a victim
accost his murderer when
there were so many?

This time, and every time, Halabja
won't move. Omar Khawar* soothes
his child—after this, every word
is excess.

Omar Khawar is weakened
by his wounds. He can't knock
on anyone's door. Please. Let him
rest in peace.

Our Holocaust

*for the flowers of the season of Anfal,
those flowers that fell in spring*

They took them after the sun's last light,
not one chance to look back
at our small village.
Anfal undid our geography, transplanted
us to the desert: a twofold tragedy.

Between the trampled flowers and warm
soil, Anfal created itself.

Desert, you be my witness: this
night, this road, in this far country
I am a stranger, my lantern dim.
The dogs of Nugra Salman Prison*
bark. I can't see. Pieces of my liver, lost
to place, to grave, litter a corner
of your charred house.

Dear desert, for the first time
our mountain waters spring up
from your dry throat. That's why
your voice is cool to my ears,
sad and sweet like a hayran.*

When they took them, the homeland
said, "My presence is the child
of their absence. Ah, each presence
is a sheaf of absence. Ah, each absence
and presence fills me with death."

From here on, women are left
without men. They wear
the night, married to vigilance.

Strange, that cycle of history: the youth
left their inheritance, the youth fled
and the elderly returned on foot
from the galaxy of Hell.

The slippers of children remain,
left behind like unripened peaches, pale plums.
The fawns: never, never again to see them.
That year was the year of Anfal, the year
of Anfal, the year when shedding blood became
halal,* the year of the genocide
of caterpillars, the season of shearing
the mountain's peak,
the season of reaping livestock,
the season of theft,
the season of invasion,
the days of falling,
the days of introducing Qaiss to Layla,* Farhad to Shirin,*
the day of releasing the evil eye,
the upside-down hour, the laughter
between flatbread and the oven,
the year the cats were abandoned
like smoke rising from a torched village,
the year mayors came nose to nose
with the scorched ones and said
in broad daylight, "Good morning,"
the year of Anfal was—ah,
ah!—the year of Anfal.

That year the faces of stones turned yellow.
Date palms like ostriches buried their heads
in cold soil, their roots groaning.
Dense smoke stung the eyes of the cactus
shimmering in the mirage. Wild flowers
became empty prayers.

When they took them, everything
faded: revolution, manners, life,
beauty. Epic poems slumped.
That history: bright sugar dissolving
in the toxic dark. The rose
surrendered, became a thistle.
The nation that forgets its Anfal
is beheaded.

Human Rights

How can I indict
the Isabelline shrike who
on gentle mornings,
busy stealing
from the farmer's field,
startles the dreams of sleepers?

Two Chairs

1.

News of my dark days:
not drunk, not dim,
they won't listen
to song. My sobbing
is their music. I laugh through

tears until, cackling,
the red creek bursts. I cry
through laughter until
I am mad, confusing happiness
for misfortune.

An optimist, am I
allowed to ask, "What do you want
from me?" Look here,
a Middle Eastern man sits
on a chair of my virtue.
He crosses his legs.
Each foot says, one hundred times,
"On my honor"—ay, the rotted honor
of a Middle Eastern man.

2.

I walk the sky. I carry
the ball of earth
in this small, heavy
head of mine.

I walk the earth
and he sits
in my head.

This chair is gold, or is it
woven strands of hair?
I don't know.

The chair's feet
penetrate my soul,
my veil—I can't sit—
it must not break—
he shatters me—
he sits—

The N's of Negative

1. Not Existence

Ah, I wish existence were a walnut.
I'd crack the skin and savor
the nut. What will you do
to existence, this most striking
bloom picked from the universe?

Will you wait for it to see you?
Brooding about its wilting
as it blossoms, its decay
as it wilts, the end
of all life as it decays?

I wish existence were
a candle. With one breath,
I would snuff it out. I wish death
were the end. Then I would die.
It's easier to desire death
than befriend life. Nobody
leaves death, but life is always
left. I wish existence
did not exist.

2. Not Loving

Clouds don't love sky. They rain
for earth. Rain doesn't love
earth. It evaporates. Sun
doesn't love man. Every night
it leaves. Moon doesn't
love man. Every day it's absent.
God doesn't love us. He chooses
some for heaven. You

don't love me. You can live
without me. You travel,
you forget. The disaster
is this: men don't love men.
They die, kill, sleep, scorn.

3. Not Able

He told me, "Shahrazad,* stop
this telling of tales.
I cannot not kill you."

4. Not Real

They left. Lucky us,
from time to time they return.
They still believe they are sons
of this family. They wear the homeland
on their feet. They sympathize
from far off. They look down
their noses and criticize, but
it is written and the soil knows:
these are not the real Kurds.

LEAF

One leaf is enough
to remind me of a line
from a friend's letter
written just before a trip:
*Each place I go I will send
you leaves.* That word:
my friends and I interpreted romance.
We thought two autumn leaves
of each country would be enveloped
and sent back with foreign postage.
But *leaf* for him was simply
dollar. Misunderstanding, a hurricane
between us, killed off
all friendship and letters,
even polite greeting.

SPEECH

"The mountain, nose high
in the air, opens its heart
to no one, claims it never
loves, refuses to laugh,
and gathers wrinkles
on its forehead. So it explodes:
its insides rush out and fire,
shaped as water, spreads."
                    —Volcano

"A revolution and nation
are like a boy and girl
as their engagement begins:
the boy strings out a long line
of lies and the girl makes shining
dreams out of those words.
Later, a revolution and nation
are the same boy and girl, but
become husband and wife.
And there start the stories
of cheating, chaos, and divorce."
                    —Political Party

A Black Wind said,
"I detest this world's
foundations. I will try
destruction for a change."
I responded, "Like you, I detest
these foundations, but I want
love as the change."
                    —Breeze

"After night, night
comes. Day, too, is

night, yet a beam
of beauty shines on,
living in it."
          —Poet

"No longer hang Kchi Kafrosh*
on me. No longer. Enough.
I understand my honor
is servant to colonization."
          —Wall of a House, Ancient and Cracked

"There was no road. I smuggled
my words. They shot at me.
My horse was wounded,
my vase of flowers fell.
They yelled, 'Who are you?'
I did not answer. I knew
that those who hold weapons
never know those who hold pens."
          —Shahrazad

"Between the Nothing Road
and No Choice, there is an old
bridge that ties this side
of our world to the other.
Brave lovers cross it
but cowards are left behind."
          —Speech

NIETZSCHE

Nietzsche said, "Women are cats.
When they breed, cows." If fate
placed that lunatic before me,
I'd say, "Even you can't know
what you're not. Give me
one night and watch me turn
you into a fool. Watch me
turn shadowed doubt
into the source of belief,
belief into a shadowed
doubting man. Give me one night,
but let it wake
to see me with a kiss
transform you from thinker
to thought."

SHORT RED SKIRT

I will bring back
an old fashion from the era
of our mothers: beautiful
short skirts. I will look through
the black and white photographs,
the albums of imagination
that exist in every home.

I don't know why the present
shies away from its past.
The world has become a better liar.

This stanza washes in dew
then, dressed in a skirt,
short and red, it wanders
among the conformed clothing
of our era, chagrined.

This stanza bares an arm,
a knee, it is narcissus and poppies
and roses. When I wear
a very short, very red skirt
you avoid me. Give me a shot glass
of tenderness. I want to get drunk.
You didn't refuse me in the light, but
you didn't die for me in the dark.

You're confused: with a sin
as grave as writing, as grave
as showing skin, how can
my heart mimic angels
and Doghdova?* You
can't believe my life

fulfills me. I want to say,
"My poetry mimics my life!"

You can't believe I am
so intimate with Life.
Death could die
for one of my kisses.

Those shocked stares
can tell you where
I have gone. When I walk
down those city streets
the catcalls surge.

With a short red skirt
I announce: "Spring has come,
open the windows.
It won't last." My tongue

is honey and sugar and syrup,
yet this era's hard heart embitters me.
Soon, a photo of winter
will appear on my calendar
and I'll be finished.
But then, another irrepressible
spring will come with its own
short red skirt.

FLOWERS IN MY HAIR

The party started.
I put all these flowers
in my hair as if I were waiting
for something. I let my yearning
eyelashes meet. When
I opened my eyes, he held another
girl's hands, dancing,
as the hands of an illusion
waited for these crazy hands
of mine to answer.

FRIDAY

Friday* is a dead day.
We sleep, we eat, we rest, more
than we need. Friday
doesn't count. I don't see you.
Friday is like a funeral—look—
the mosques call the men,
the graveyards, the women.
The day shouldn't exist.
We relive our losses. Criminals
plan. Our lovers
are lonely.

MY LOVER

My lover didn't dig
into Behistun Mountain or give
his feet to the desert for me.
From Istanbul, he wrote poems
only for the eye of our homeland.
He is not Farhad, not Nali, not Majnoon,*
but by today's standards, he is
a knight in love's army, the Shah
of love because he burrowed into
my heart to help the soil breathe.
In an age of death and departure
he makes poems and laughter his home.

SOCKS

Traffic police stop the car
I'm in and ask, "Why don't you
write poems now?" The scented letters
of peshmerga on the front lines,
the hands at work in the publishing house
all say, "Why haven't your poems
appeared?" In dismal alleys,
children playing house
say, "Why don't you look
like you did before?" I hear
the gossip of writers
and smugglers, martyrs
and prisoners. If Dlawar's* broad calm
were my heart and Jamal's* patience
seeped from my soul, I would call
all Kurds this evening
to the front gate of the sacred
school of poetry. I would answer
them, "The stench of socks
keeps me from writing."

TEA

You know?
A rotten poem
is like rotten tea.
You never drink it up.

Two Lives

She's no longer
narrow-waisted like handfuls
of other girls. She has forgotten
how to sashay. She is afraid to ride
the Ferris wheel and the swinging boat
of Sarchinar* as she used to
during her engagement.

She is now two lives and so, more
beautiful than the girls around her.
Men in the evenings walk by
as she worries. Among all
the women of the neighborhood,
her form is the most alluring
and also the most alive.
The sight of her belly
makes people hunger
for fresh watermelon.

While knitting socks
and a small sweater
she sees the face of her baby.
She no longer has a waist
like a shimshal.*
She's past the age
of skirts, leggings
and denim. Lipstick and high heels,
mirrors, lingerie and swimsuits,
are not worn by the body
in this state. From now on,
she speaks to what's inside.
She's not aware of us.

God, may you spread goodness
over the nine months she lives
in the neighborhood
of Life and Death. God,
may you spread goodness
over the preordained road
women travel.

GULLIBLE LOVER

Today, as usual, my mother
placed the skin of an onion*
on her head and said, "Ay,
onion, don't make me cry. I will
marry you. You look as if
a bald one watered you. You sting."

How my heart stirs
for the onion: always it is
duped. Before the hour
of execution, a typical woman
swears love to the onion.
This gullible lover bows
his head before the knife
of his beloved, a liar
who kills him with love.

Excerpt from the Story of My Heart

Ah, it begins
with a cry what begins
from our mothers.
To tell the story of the rose
I tend in my heart I must
go into the howling storm,
I must get wet.

Faced with icy existence, I must move
my mouth. You know
as my lips move what I want
to say. I exist entirely
in the movement of my lips.

Crying is philosophy, not a weapon
among women, not an ever-flowing fountainhead
of forgiveness. Of all beings,
we have wept most. Our friends stand
under the waterfall of our tears, as do
our enemies. Our homeland is soaked
like our lands of exile.

I don't know how to return
to a story I've always wanted
to forget, how to throw myself
against the soliloquy of a heart
that taught flowers patience
and hosted universal injustices,
a heart whose worst sin
is that it grew in the shape
of a rose, that it lived and wilted
as a rose.

My heart is not content
that my beloved, my poetry, and my fate
call me a butterfly.
When I run my hands over my body, I feel
spurs, thorns, and spines.

No, I don't want to turn to dust,
I don't want to die young or
be easily caught.

Why do I even have these two wings
when I desire no place?
Damned be those days I dressed
in transparent wings and raised them high,
so high I couldn't tell whether
those who stung me
were humans or wasps.
What do I do with these wings?
I think like a rose, not a dog.
These senses, what are they good for?
I live addicted to flight.

After weeping, my heart shakes,
as on the dim, cold, winter night when
my little brother and I, in mismatched boots,
threw Komala's political leaflets
into people's damp front yards.
We rolled home like two beads.
Before our gate, we would take
a deep breath, scared of nothing
but our mother's anger. "Where were you,"
she would say, "on a night like this?"
During those times, we thought
like roses and lived like butterflies,

we were real as Saholaka and
dreamy as Sarchinar. These days,
we are butterflies ground to dust,
we are cut flowers.

On a page of this heart, imprisoned
and protesting, it is written:
My dear, my government, you
are busy celebrating with the old
and feeble in the receiving rooms
of tribes. You are drunk with grasping
the sterile and wrinkled hands
of this tribe and that tribe.
You barely recognize these hands
about to despair and migrate. Now,
in this trying season, you are far
from the heat of young hearts, so far
you can't decipher the handwriting
of their protest. You can't read
the new alphabet of this generation's
murdered dreams and desires.

Don't dream, my government,
my heart's government. At times,
your bright thoughts are overwhelmed
by the suicide bomber who can't discuss
an ounce of his heart's disease. Then,
at times, the conversation runs over
pages and pages.
Don't dream, my government,
most beautiful, most endearing
of all the world's governments.

Why build these walls?
I am not a smuggler, but a poet.
At every checkpoint, you search me.

Don't despair, government of my eyes.
It is written: may your neck be free.
What more can we say?

Ah, to this day,
all expression ends
in bitterness. It seems
my heart doesn't know how to hold
other hearts. The language
of smooth balm and many meanings
of each letter: I can't find it.
More, I don't want it.

I have not yet written
this story of mine on these
small pages, these wavering lines.
I need a different tongue. I don't dare…
I am too depressed to touch
anything new. I am ashamed
to knock on today's door
with this old story.
I can't hold my head high
like those arrogant in their ignorance.
I can't enter without
distress, my beating heart, burdens.

Ah, the end begins
in a cry. My heart is finished,
but the stories continue.
I will stomp on my heart
if I can change nothing—
these encounters, my fate, this fate
that has suppressed earth and sky.
No, I won't finish this telling just yet.

A Fruit Seller's Philosophy

My friend, you are an apricot.
I want to taste you, but
not your core.

My old friend, sometimes
you are a tangerine: all on your own,
you get naked. Sometimes an apple,
with skin, without skin, you end up
in my mouth.

You, my neighbor,
are a fruit knife.
Every time our family
sits to eat, there
you are. Forgive me,
I don't like you.

My dear homeland, you
are a lemon: at your name
the world's mouth wells up.
Shivers come over me.

Oh, stranger,
you are a watermelon.
Until I dig into your guts with a knife,
I cannot know who you are.

Notes

Becoming a Martyr—This poem echoes with its nothingness. No flowers, no kisses, no tears, no miseries, no candy at the funeral, no financial or heavenly incentives. The speaker commands the bereaved to bear nothing. She wants nothing.

The emptiness resounds in each line's negation: "I want no." At the end of four of the last six lines, "nothing" tolls like a bell. This nothing is a cousin to the winter of Stevens' "Snowman," the wintering to which Rilke invites Orpheus. Ahmad as a martyr has a mind of winter; she chooses to be ahead of all parting. Yet Ahmad's character, the martyr, is not alone in a forest clearing nor is she mourning a lost lover. She is a political figure.

As Abdulla Pashew, another famous Kurdish poet, has said, "The poet is more than a poet in Kurdistan." Unlike in America, where the poet seems to belong mostly to other poets, Kurdish poets are public figures. Every personal choice means something. No personal choice is private.

What Ahmad wants is to be a moment of nothing in this crowd of competing desires.

She uses the definition poem to re-conceive the politicized religious concept of "martyr." Were she to choose that death— lovely subjunctive—she would reject the offered incentives: forgiveness for all sin, eternal life in paradise, virgins in heaven, and financial assistance to the family left behind. The poet transgresses against the tradition of martyrdom. Not only does she want nothing, she commands those she leaves behind to cherish nothing as her final gift. Through gratitude, not anger, the poet transgresses against the tradition of martyrdom. She is replete. That is her revolution.

BUTTONS—The intimacy in "Buttons" is small, like the poem itself. A reader, especially a Western reader, could easily miss it. For certain audiences, a kiss is no longer scandalous, only an innocent beginning to adulthood and sexuality. A reader learns much in the poet's opening assertion: the kisses that caused this poem were innocent. She almost undercuts her first line in her second. What kind of kiss is so innocent it causes buttons to fall off? In a clever elision of the actors, the syntax places the blame on the buttons.

The poet introduces a woman, the speaker's mother, in the act of repair. This repair is more a cover-up operation. No one must know about the fallen button. There is much at risk here: her daughter's honor, the family's. So, the mother stitches. The daughter, in trouble, watching, sits beside her as she sews. Without bothering to look up, the mother sees the urge to watch and write, knows its danger, and warns her daughter off.

The first intimacy is only implied. The reader never sees the lover. The second intimacy, caused by the first, is a mother and daughter, a subject and a writer, rebelliously complicit in both the act of love and the poem. Love and the poem exist only illicitly.

Only once in three years have I witnessed a mundane moment of womanhood. A family of a musician I'd befriended invited me to their mountain home for dinner. In sight of Iran's border crossing, we boiled the rice Kurdish-style. The pot, bigger than the circumference of my arms, sat suspended over the open fire by two cinderblocks. The musician's mother taught me the word for "raisin." Qshmish. Delighted by the childlike sound, I teased that I would name my child that just so I could say it every day. They laughed and piled my rice high with roasted almonds and qshmish. After we had done dishes, as we served tea and sat around the warmth of the kettle, the women of the family fell to discussing hair removal.

Universal girl talk. Where did the daughter-in-law go
for her arms? Her moustache? After three years of being a
constant guest, held at a certain distance, this intimacy was
tender, the inclusion sweet. I didn't know I had a moustache.
They informed me, just a small one. And had I ever considered
my eyebrows?

Moments like these punctuate the daily relationships and desires
of every woman. It is an act of bravery to kiss, just as it is to
write the kiss. But it takes subtle courage to focus the poem on
the mother, on one generation of women confronting another's
changing definitions of innocence and honesty. There is love;
there is threat. What does motherly love look like in a society
that continues to prize virginity and sexual seclusion? Preventing
the tryst or hiding the aftermath? How should a wife and
mother preserve her family's honor? Stone the child or obscure
the evidence?

Each generation answers these questions differently. As we
translated this poem together, Darya and I got talking—about
womanhood, our separate struggles to understand and define
the word, what meaning the word takes on in Iraq. She told me
a friend of hers was afraid to go home. In her village, a woman
made rounds of the neighborhoods, equipped to perform female
genital mutilation. Neither her mother nor her aunt would call
the woman into their houses. One day, when her cousins were
home, her aunt away, their grandmother took the opportunity.

Kajal portrays a gentle moment of this confrontation. She
defines audacity not in having sought a kiss, but in declaring it
sinless and bringing the missing button home to Mom. Mom,
however threatening, sews the button back in place. The poem
hints toward its wide margins: space where definitions can shift
and family can be safe haven.

COUNTRY OF TERROR—In Sulaimani, Iraq, the city where Ahmad
grew up, men use the street as one long café. Handcarts sell hot
tea, sandwiches, and nuts roasted by blowtorch in steel tumblers.
Men congregate for meals, standing in clusters around the carts
or squatting curbside. Some build improvised shelters from
scraps around the road. There, on worn and dusty couches or
folding chairs or woven mats, they sit in the shade and smoke.
In Saholaka, a district in the city named for a long-shuttered ice
factory, men spill into the streets, blocking traffic as they wander
past the carts and pop-up music shops. Women when they are on
the road are in motion. The street is a line of transit to them, not a
community.

Ahmad, in her poem, re-envisions that territory. She shows the
street beneath the men. She turns her poem over to the street's
speech. She claims that space, putting her own name on the
street signs. In Sulaimani, the streets bear the names of classical
Kurdish poets who have come before her. Why not hers, she asks.

The street that carries her name will be quiet as a poem's house and
raucous as her insides. Lips within lips. The original phrase is, "Lip
of lips." The metaphor indicates voice and fullness. Within one
voice, there is another and another and another. As a reader, I
can't help but hear a reference to other lips, to another fullness.
While this may be over-reading, Kurdish is a language of the
body. "Forgive" is "free your neck." "Confess" is "tread on your
teeth." A common greeting is "I put you above my eyes." Children,
when referred to affectionately, are those who "eat your liver."

It might have been clearer to translate "lip of lips" as, "How full is a
human being?" This exact line lived in the translation for months.
In the end, the metaphor and image found their way back in.

In the following stanza, Ahmad moves the reader between the
street she desires and the reality. There are plenty of stories of the
real-life terror visited upon women, which women pass along.

Some may be urban legends while others are captured on smart phones and uploaded to YouTube. How many have I heard myself? Recently, a rumor circulated about a girl, her father's favorite, who didn't ask his permission before agreeing to marry the man she loved. Her father initially relented. Then, pressured by family members, he walked into her room as she slept and shot her. Another: the story of the young girl stoned to death by her town for having married in secret a boy of another religion. Let her street be flawless, Ahmad prays, as flawless, as pure, as the women who have died unjustly. Let her street be long, she prays, as long as their agony. It is the two-faced coin of the women she has known and the woman she is: desire and agony. Ahmad's country, Kurdistan: a country that isn't a country, has known many terrors. Today, a terror that is new, but not new, has come to the Kurdish region.

The Islamic State of Iraq and Syria (ISIS) has changed the balance of power in Iraq, in Syria, and in the broader region of the Middle East. Some Kurds see this as an opportune moment to achieve independence from their various states: Syria, Iraq, Iran, and Turkey. They do not wish to live under the Sunni extremism of ISIS or, south of the regions ISIS controls, the lesser Shiite fundamentalism that threatens. As Kurds try to work together across political, linguistic, and cultural differences that have been embedded in them by centuries of oppressive regimes, fault lines become evident.

While this poem was written long before ISIS's rise to power, the conclusion of this poem could easily describe the current conflict. The poem closes by questioning the trust Kurds bear for each other, "The quatrains of Nishapur," an ancient city in what is now northeastern Iran (a Kurdish area), "Will not suddenly trust themselves / And madly drunk with love / Walk arm in arm with me." The verses of Iranian Kurds, written in a different dialect, with hundreds of years of divergent history, will not, overnight, reveal themselves to her: an Iraqi Kurd. The poem ends in uncertainty. The poem ends without end, "We are all travelers / But I will remain a traveler."

Mirror—Terror is a pattern in the mind. It takes time to teach; it is painful to learn. The mirror of Ahmad's era shattered because it reflected the inverted values of dictatorship. Those who were small in heart, the mirror rendered tall in stature. Those who offered the largess of acceptance were brought low. Those who weren't persecuted were taught fear. Those who were persecuted were taught fear. The lessons don't die with the teacher.

Mewan grew up in many homes. Her family, politically significant, was hunted by Saddam Hussein, but also by fellow Kurds: rival political parties. The family moved city to city within the KRG, even seeking asylum in Iran, until they found a lasting haven in Holland. Mewan, whose name translates as "Visitor," grew up in that safety and returned to the semi-autonomous Kurdish region during its golden decade: a ten-year period of unprecedented security and economic prosperity. Her mother would scold her when she came home with lots of new clothes or when she would try to decorate their home. These things can all burn. We never know when we'll have to run.

Mewan had been sheltered from the lessons her mother had learned. She tried to tell her mother, "Things have changed now. It's safe now." She gently teased her mother about fears she considered outdated. Then, Daesh arrived without warning and with tremendous speed and devastation. The mirror Mewan had been holding, it shattered.

Now, she understands her mother. She wonders if there will come a day she will regret not learning to load and fire a Kalashnikov. The lessons of terror run deep. Today's Kurds fight to un-learn them.

At the university, I taught poetry writing, literary translation, and ENG 102: Critical Reading and Writing. At various levels of skill and interest, I taught students how to be awake as they read: to their own responses to the text, to the other imagination that made the text, to the community that has formed around the text.

What do you hate? What do you love? Why?

Can you articulate, without embedding your own prejudice, what the text says?

What have other readers said about this text? How are they talking to each other? How do you assess their perspectives?

Dry as it may sound, these foundational skills of the academy are groundbreaking in Iraq. The idea of "just you and the text" is virtually non-existent in that education system. Desperate students have bluntly asked what I want to hear, or, barring that, what the experts say so they can regurgitate. There is such a deep history of interpretation it has become suffocating. Poetry books designed for popular consumption come with extensive footnotes on each page, sometimes taking up more than half the folio. What should be a rich intellectual community for emerging readers and writers to join sits as a yoke on their shoulders.

Teaching students to read a text for themselves is, small as it is, teaching students to see the world for themselves. Helping students argue with rather than at their fellow students, contained to the classroom as it may be, is helping them choose empathy even in moments of stress, helping them un-learn certain lessons terror taught them.

A 102 student of mine came into my class wearing the ankle-length pants and full beard of a conservative Muslim man. He didn't participate in the class discussions. His papers were bursting with energy and quotations from whatever text we read, but lacked any framing thoughts of his own. After class, I finally asked him why the disconnect. He said simply, "I don't think you really want to hear what I have to say."

He knew I was liberal. A woman. Western. He figured, better to leave well enough alone. Pass the class. Move on. I answered honestly. His ideas were important to the fullness of our conversations. Whether or not I personally agreed with him was not important. He began contributing. Stammering at first, he grew more sure of himself as I failed to descend on his opinions with the fury he anticipated.

One day, as we discussed cultural relativism, he said, "Women in America are raped more because of the way they dress." Rage surged against my eyelids. A barrage of no's lined up on my tongue. But if instinct is an itch, that day, I stopped myself from scratching. What an interesting hypothesis, I said. Let's look at its assumptions, I said. What do statistics tell us from America? We found answers. What do statistics tell us from Iraq. We found none.

It was at this point that a young veiled woman erupted. "Because we don't have any! And even if people tried to ask, no one would tell them!" The young man paused and considered.

The young woman came to me after the class. "I can't take it," she said. "He drives me absolutely crazy. Talking to him is like running your head into a brick wall, but brick must sometimes move. He never does!"

I asked her if she'd rather this young man be somewhere else, somewhere beyond our discussions. She thought, nodded, and said no.

Glossary

ANFAL: shorthand for Saddam Hussein's Anfal Campaign (1986-1989), launched toward the conclusion of the Iran-Iraq War (1980-1988). Genocidal in scope, this ethnic slaughter aimed to kill all Kurdish men of military age as well as uproot the Kurdish people with forced migration, forced Arabization, and the complete destruction of over 4,000 Kurdish villages.

BABA: affectionate term for "father."

DLAWAR QARADAGHI: contemporary Kurdish poet (1963-) and friend of Kajal Ahmad's, Qaradaghi studied drama at the Institute of Fine Arts in Baghdad and has published nine collections of poetry as well as translations of novels, biographies, and plays from Arabic, Persian, and Swedish into Kurdish. Though currently living in Sulaimani, the poet lived for a time in exile in Sweden.

DOGHDOVA: Mother of Zarathustra, the Zoroastrian prophet.

FIND, FIND, FIND: Kurdish folk wisdom: when you have lost an object, sing this proverb to have it returned to you, "Find, find, find it for me. It's not mine, it's the Divine's."

FRIDAY: Sabbath day of Islam and the weekend's beginning in most Middle Eastern countries.

HALABJA: as part of the Anfal Campaign (1986-1989), conventional and chemical weapons were deployed against Halabja. Tabun, sarin, VX, and mustard gases were spread across the city, killing 5,000 people immediately and injuring as many or more. Halabja now falls within the borders of the semi-autonomous Kurdish Regional Government (KRG) and hosts a museum commemorating the tragedies of 1988.

HALAL: Arabic for "permissible." For instance, food that has been prepared in accordance with Islamic law is halal.

HAMA DOK: main character from Yeshar Kemal's novel, *Hama Dok*.

HANDFUL OF SALT: Kurdish folk wisdom: place a handful of salt in the shoes of a guest who has overstayed. It is a host's subtle signal for the guest to leave.

HAYRAN: specific type of Kurdish song.

HIS SHOES: Kurdish folk wisdom: you will travel whatever direction your shoes face when you take them off.

JAMAL XAMBAR: a contemporary Kurdish poet (1962-) and friend of Kajal Ahmad's. Xambar, born Jamal Amin, earned his law degree from the University of Baghdad in 1984 and was employed as a lawyer for eleven years in the KRG. He migrated to Australia in 2002 and became an Australian citizen in 2004. He has published four collections of poetry and has translated four books into Kurdish. He recently returned to the KRG.

JAMANA: a traditional and distinctive black and white patterned scarf wrapped around and securing a Kurdish hat.

KHUNIGAR: a Kurdish singer.

KCHI KAFROSH: literally translated, this means, "The Daughter of Kafrosh." Kchi Kafrosh, the story goes, was a beautiful girl who was stolen from her family by a British officer. Her painting has become the Mona Lisa of Kurdish culture.

KOMALA: a Marxist-Leninist predecessor to the PUK (the Patriotic Union of Kurdistan), one of three major political parties in the KRG (Kurdish Regional Government) of Iraq.

LAYLA AND QAISS: In folklore, a boy named Qaiss falls in love with a girl named Layla. Her father forbids the two to marry. Obsessed by his love for her, Qaiss pursues her, earning the name *Majnoon*, or "Possessed." When she marries another, Majnoon flees to the desert where he writes poems in the shifting sand.

MAJNOON: See LAYLA AND QAISS (above).

MULLAH: title designating a local Muslim cleric or leader educated in Islamic theology and law.

NALI: Kurdish poet, linguist, and translator (1797-1856) credited with his era's renaissance of the Kurdish language.

NISHAPUR: historic capital of Khorasan, the northeastern Kurdish region of Iran.

NUGRA SALMAN PRISON: or *Nigret Al Salman*, "the Pit of Salman," was a desert prison camp used to hold Kurdish political prisoners—men, women, and children—during the Anfal Campaign. Here they were systematically starved to death. Bodies of the dead were fed to the prison dogs within sight of the prisoners. The prison was active before and after Anfal.

OMAR KHAWAR: Halabja, the city at the center of the 1988 chemical bombings, found its symbol in Omar Khawar, a victim who died cradling his infant son.

SAHOLAKA: district in Sulaimani originally known for its production of ice, now famous for its evening markets of street food and music.

SARCHINAR: district in Sulaimani known for its amusement parks and casual restaurants.

SHAHRAZAD: or Scheherazade: queen and storyteller of *A Thousand and One Nights*.

SHAHRIYAR: fictional king whose wife, Scheherazade, told stories to stay alive.

SHARIA: Islamic law.

SHIMSHAL: a type of flute.

SHIRIN AND FARHAD: Farhad and Shirin are characters in the epic Persian poem *The Shahnameh*, or "The Book of Kings." A sculptor, Farhad falls in love with Shirin, a princess. Khosrow, Shirin's suitor and a prince, exiles Farhad to Behistun Mountain to carve stairs into the cliffs. At the false news of Shirin's death, Farhad kills himself by leaping from the mountain.

SINGLE STRAND: Kurdish folk wisdom: when a single strand of hair falls into your face, kiss it and touch it to your eyes. Then, you will see the one you love.

SIRAT: the Sirat Bridge connects this life to Paradise and is a hair-thin construction that each soul must walk.

SKIN OF AN ONION: Kurdish folk wisdom: if you place the skin of an onion on your head and promise to marry him, he won't make you cry as you chop him up.

TUNI BABA: a labyrinthine area in the city of Sulaimani.

About the Author

Kajal Ahmad was born in 1967 in Kirkuk, a disputed city in Iraq with a strong Kurdish population. A poet, journalist, and social critic, she has published four books: *Benderî Bermoda* (1999), *Wutekanî Wutin* (1999), *Qaweyek le gel ev da* (2001), and *Awênem şikand* (2004). Ahmad worked for over a decade as the Editor-in-Chief of *Kurdistani Nwe* and at times has worked as a TV host for KurdSat. She now lives in Sulaimani.

About the Artist

Kurdish artist Lukman Ahmad, from Al Hasakah, Syria, came to the United States in 2010. His work reflects his personal connection to Kurdish spirit and identity. Currently he is a broadcaster at the Voice of America, Kurdish Services. He has exhibited in more than 45 countries, including Syria, Turkey, Switzerland, Lebanon, and the United States. He is a member of the Arlington Arts Gallery and lives in Virginia. More work can be seen at www.lukmanahmad.net.

ABOUT THE TRANSLATORS

ALANA MARIE LEVINSON-LABROSSE served as the Founding
Chair of the English Department at the American University
of Iraq, Sulaimani (AUIS), where she taught for four years,
covering composition, literary translation, and poetry writing.
She received her MFA at Warren Wilson and an MEd from
the University of Virginia. Individual translations and non-
fiction articles have appeared in *The Iowa Review*, *Words Without
Borders*, Poetry Society of America, *The Fair Observer*, the Iowa
International Writing Program's online gallery, and the anthology
SoJust. She is currently a Non-Residential Fellow at AUIS'
Institute for Regional and International Studies (IRIS) and a PhD
candidate at the University of Exeter's Centre for Kurdish Studies.

DARYA ABDUL-KARIM ALI NAJM graduated in 2014 from
the American University of Iraq, Sulaimani, with a major in
International Studies and a minor in English Literature. She is a
native of Sulaimani, the city many call "the cultural capital" of the
KRG (Kurdish Regional Government). Issues of womanhood in
Kurdish literature interest her greatly; years ago she fell in love
with the bold, yet vulnerable voice of Kajal Ahmad. Currently, she
works as the Marketing Manager at Suli Media, an advertising
agency, but plans to resume her studies of literature and politics
within the year.

MEWAN NAHRO SAID SOFI is a Masters candidate in
Management of Governance Networks at Erasmus University in
Rotterdam. She graduated in 2015 from the American University
of Iraq, Sulaimani, with a major in International Studies. She is
originally from Erbil, but was born in Iran and spent most of her
childhood in the Netherlands. She is an advocate for Kurdistan and
women's rights. She began translating Ahmad because she sees her
own values resonating in Ahmad's poetry.

BARBARA GOLDBERG received an MFA from American University, Washington, D.C., and is the author of five prize-winning poetry books: *The Royal Baker's Daughter* (recipient of the Felix Pollak Poetry Award), *Kingdom of Speculation, Marvelous Pursuits, Cautionary Tales,* and *Berta Broadfoot and Pepin the Short.* Goldberg is also a prolific translator. Her newest book of translations is *Scorched by the Sun: Poems by Moshe Dor,* supported by the Institute for the Translation of Hebrew Literature. Goldberg and Dor translated and edited *The Fire Stays in Red: Poems by Ronny Someck* as well as four anthologies of contemporary Israeli poets. She is the recipient of two fellowships from the National Endowment for the Arts, five individual artist's grants from the Maryland State Arts Council, as well as the Armand G. Erpf Award from the Translation Center at Columbia University. She is currently Series Editor of The Word Works International Editions and lives in Chevy Chase, Maryland.

About The Word Works

The Word Works, a nonprofit literary organization, publishes contemporary poetry and presents public programs. Imprints include the the Hilary Tham Capital Collection, The Washington Prize, International Editions, and The Tenth Gate Prize. A reading period is also held in May.

Monthly, The Word Works offers free literary programs in the Chevy Chase, MD, Café Muse series, and each summer, it holds free poetry programs in Washington, D.C.'s Rock Creek Park. Annually in June, two high school students debut in the Joaquin Miller Poetry Series as winners of the Jacklyn Potter Young Poets Competition. Since 1974, Word Works programs have included: "In the Shadow of the Capitol," a symposium and archival project on the African American intellectual community in segregated Washington, D.C.; the Gunston Arts Center Poetry Series; the Poet Editor panel discussions at The Writer's Center; and Master Class workshops.

As a 501(c)3 organization, The Word Works has received awards from the National Endowment for the Arts, the National Endowment for the Humanities, the D.C. Commission on the Arts & Humanities, the Witter Bynner Foundation, Poets & Writers, The Writer's Center, Bell Atlantic, the David G. Taft Foundation, and others, including many generous private patrons.

The Word Works has established an archive of artistic and administrative materials in the Washington Writing Archive housed in the George Washington University Gelman Library. It is a member of the Council of Literary Magazines and Presses and its books are distributed by Small Press Distribution.

wordworksbooks.org

OTHER WORD WORKS BOOKS

Karren L. Alenier, *Wandering on the Outside*
Karren L. Alenier & Miles David Moore, eds., *Winners: A Retrospective of the Washington Prize*
Karren L. Alenier, ed., *Whose Woods These Are*
Christopher Bursk, ed., *Cool Fire*
Barbara Goldberg, *Berta Broadfoot and Pepin the Short*
Frannie Lindsay, *If Mercy*
Marilyn McCabe, *Glass Factory*
W.T. Pfefferle, *My Coolest Shirt*
Ayaz Pirani, *Happy You Are Here*
Jacklyn Potter, Dwaine Rieves, Gary Stein, eds., *Cabin Fever: Poets at Joaquin Miller's Cabin*
Robert Sargent, *Aspects of a Southern Story & A Woman from Memphis*
Nancy White, ed., *Word for Word*

International Editions

Keyne Cheshire (trans.), *Murder at Jagged Rock: A Tragedy by Sophocles*
Yoko Danno & James C. Hopkins, *The Blue Door*
Moshe Dor, Barbara Goldberg, Giora Leshem, eds., *The Stones Remember: Native Israeli Poets*
Moshe Dor (Barbara Goldberg, trans.), *Scorched by the Sun*
Lee Sang (Myong-Hee Kim, trans.), *Crow's Eye View: The Infamy of Lee Sang, Korean Poet*
Vladimir Levchev (Henry Taylor, trans.), *Black Book of the Endangered Species*

The Tenth Gate Prize

Jennifer Barber, *Works on Paper*, 2015
Lisa Sewell, *Impossible Object*, 2014

The Hilary Tham Capital Collection

Mel Belin, *Flesh That Was Chrysalis*

Carrie Bennett, *The Land Is a Painted Thing*

Doris Brody, *Judging the Distance*

Sarah Browning, *Whiskey in the Garden of Eden*

Grace Cavalieri, *Pinecrest Rest Haven*

Cheryl Clarke, *By My Precise Haircut*

Christopher Conlon, *Gilbert and Garbo in Love*
    & *Mary Falls: Requiem for Mrs. Surratt*

Donna Denizé, *Broken like Job*

W. Perry Epes, *Nothing Happened*

Bernadette Geyer, *The Scabbard of Her Throat*

Barbara G. S. Hagerty, *Twinzilla*

James Hopkins, *Eight Pale Women*

Brandon Johnson, *Love's Skin*

Marilyn McCabe, *Perpetual Motion*

Judith McCombs, *The Habit of Fire*

James McEwen, *Snake Country*

Miles David Moore, *The Bears of Paris* & *Rollercoaster*

Kathi Morrison-Taylor, *By the Nest*

Tera Vale Ragan, *Reading the Ground*

Michael Shaffner, *The Good Opinion of Squirrels*

Maria Terrone, *The Bodies We Were Loaned*

Hilary Tham, *Bad Names for Women*
    & *Counting*

Barbara Louise Ungar, *Charlotte Brontë, You Ruined My Life*
    & *Immortal Medusa*

Jonathan Vaile, *Blue Cowboy*

Rosemary Winslow, *Green Bodies*

Michele Wolf, *Immersion*

Joe Zealberg, *Covalence*

The Washington Prize

Nathalie F. Anderson, *Following Fred Astaire*, 1998

Michael Atkinson, *One Hundred Children Waiting for a Train*, 2001

Molly Bashaw, *The Whole Field Still Moving Inside It*, 2013

Carrie Bennett, *biography of water*, 2004

Peter Blair, *Last Heat*, 1999

John Bradley, *Love-in-Idleness: The Poetry of Roberto Zingarello*, 1995, 2nd edition 2014

Christopher Bursk, *The Way Water Rubs Stone*, 1988

Richard Carr, *Ace*, 2008

Jamison Crabtree, *Rel[AM]ent*, 2014

Barbara Duffey, *Simple Machines*, 2015

B. K. Fischer, *St. Rage's Vault*, 2012

Linda Lee Harper, *Toward Desire*, 1995

Ann Rae Jonas, *A Diamond Is Hard But Not Tough*, 1997

Frannie Lindsay, *Mayweed*, 2009

Richard Lyons, *Fleur Carnivore*, 2005

Elaine Magarrell, *Blameless Lives*, 1991

Fred Marchant, *Tipping Point*, 1993, 2nd edition 2013

Ron Mohring, *Survivable World*, 2003

Barbara Moore, *Farewell to the Body*, 1990

Brad Richard, *Motion Studies*, 2010

Jay Rogoff, *The Cutoff*, 1994

Prartho Sereno, *Call from Paris*, 2007, 2nd edition 2013

Enid Shomer, *Stalking the Florida Panther*, 1987

John Surowiecki, *The Hat City After Men Stopped Wearing Hats*, 2006

Miles Waggener, *Phoenix Suites*, 2002

Charlotte Warren, *Gandhi's Lap*, 2000

Mike White, *How to Make a Bird with Two Hands*, 2011

Nancy White, *Sun, Moon, Salt*, 1992, 2nd edition 2010

George Young, *Spinoza's Mouse*, 1996

CPSIA information can be obtained
at www.ICGtesting.com
Printed in the USA
FFOW02n1610210716
26122FF